Power Write!

Power Write!

A Practical Guide to Words That Work

Helene Hinis

SkillPath Publications
Mission, KS

Editor: Kelly Scanlon

Page Layout and Cover Design: Rod Hankins

Library of Congress Catalog Card Number: 95-71727

ISBN: 1-878542-00-1

10 9 8   06 07 08 09

Printed in the United States of America

For
Georgia and Christopher,
Urania and William,
Eleni and Kyriako

And for Antoni

Contents

Before
You
Start...

The process of writing involves much more than cranking out ideas on a page. Before you ever put your pen to paper or fingers on the keyboard, you must know three essential things: your subject, your readers, and yourself.

Know Your Subject

How well do you have to know your subject before you can begin writing about it? Well enough to explain it to someone unfamiliar with the field. The more you know about your subject, the easier it will be to write about it.

There are a number of ways you can gain information about your subject:

- Firsthand personal experience
- Interviews
- Research

Know Your Readers

The better you know your readers, the more ways you have to influence them. Ask yourself:

- How does my reader think?
- How does my reader feel?
- What motivates my reader?
- What are my reader's biases?
- What does my reader know?
- What does my reader need to know?
- What interests my reader?
- What will help my reader understand?
- When does my reader need this information?

Know Yourself

Think of yourself as a writer. Writers are people who create order out of chaos and make what they have to say clear to others. Your job is to communicate and, to communicate effectively, you have to be yourself—your real self. The person the reader wants to hear from is the person he or she talked to on the phone or met for lunch, not some artificial, detached "professional" who writes like he or she thinks writing should be. Your voice and your manners are what got you where you are—use them.

1

Putting Your Ideas on Paper

Getting Started

For most people, the hardest part about writing is getting started. Once you get the first few words down, you're on our way, but those first words are the toughest. Here's how to get them on the page sooner.

Avoid Interruptions

Writing isn't typing. When you're interrupted while you're writing, you can't just pick up where you left off. You have to go through the terrible process of starting all over again. The fewer the interruptions, the fewer times you have to start again. That's time and energy saved that you can devote to other tasks.

Do All Your Writing at One Time

Some people tend to answer a letter right away—while it's fresh in their minds—or at least at the first chance they get. As a result, most people engage in two or three writing sessions during the course of a day. That's two or three times you have to go through the trouble of getting started. Let those writing assignments pile up. If you're a morning person, complete them all in the morning; if you're an afternoon person, complete them all in the afternoon. That way you have to get started only once. You can devote the time and energy you have saved to other tasks.

Do the Easy Stuff First

Ernest Hemingway used to begin every working day by writing two letters to friends. Once he had warmed up with the letters, he was ready to begin work on a short story or novel. Following Hemingway's example, write your easy memos and letters first. Then, once you're warmed up, you can move on to your more difficult writing tasks.

Say It to Someone Else

Having a hard time making what you want to say clear? Say it to a friend or colleague. Because most people are so much better at speaking than writing, what you say will probably come out pretty close to perfect the first time.

Write to Someone Else

If you do not know the person you are writing to or are having a hard time crossing the impersonal barrier that separates you from your reader, pretend you are writing to someone you do know. That will help you get started faster and write closer to your natural writing voice.

Break the Material Down

Are you inundated with more thoughts than you can handle? Write each one down on a 3-by-5 card. Then lay the cards out where you can see them all at once. Each card, each idea, stands for a separate paragraph in whatever you're writing. Decide the order in which to present your ideas.

Do Something Different

Sometimes people get stuck in a routine without realizing it. If you usually write in the morning, try writing in the afternoon. If you usually work on a computer, try writing on paper. If you usually write on white paper, try yellow.

Give Up

Sometimes, no matter how hard you try, the words just won't come. Trying to force them out only works against you. So take a break. Do something mindless. In fact, the more mindless the task, the better the chance that you'll suddenly overcome that writer's block.

Mindmapping

The fastest, easiest, most effective way to generate ideas and put them on paper is through mindmapping.

The traditional way to create, organize, and record thoughts is to outline them using numbers or letters. The trouble with this method is that people's minds don't work in outlines. Mindmapping, however, works the way our minds work. It enables our thoughts to emerge naturally, without pressure or constraints.

Mindmapping also allows you to record your thoughts in a clear, logical way. All you need to do it is a piece of paper and a pencil:

Step 1: In the middle of a blank piece of paper, write the name of what you want to write about.

Step 2: Draw a circle around the name of the person, place, product, service, or idea that you have written in the center of the page.

Step 3: Sit back and relax. Don't try to force your thoughts. Most of the time you know what you're trying to say. As each thought occurs to you, record it on the page. Then circle the thought and connect it with the one that led to it.

Don't worry about being logical or correct. Your mindmap has to make sense only to you. And don't worry if you feel you're wandering aimlessly—it's just your conditioned desire to want to see everything in terms of an outline. In fact, the fewer controls you impose on your mindmap, the greater the possibilities for more creative solutions to your problems.

Organizing Your Ideas

Once you have mapped your ideas on a piece of paper, you're ready to arrange them into an outline.

Try to see each set of circles as a separate paragraph. Mark with a letter "B" the set of thoughts you want to begin with, the one you think is the most important, the one you want your reader to most remember. Then mark the second most important set of circles, the set you want to end with, with the letter "E." Now order all the other sets of circles in between. What you now have is an outline for what you are writing.

You can write directly from the outline you have created from your mindmap or, if the mindmap has become too complex to handle easily, you can list your points in traditional outline form as in the following example:

B. It's fast.

2. It's easy. You don't have to be logical, you don't have to worry about making a mistake, you don't have to worry about spelling, punctuation or grammar.

3. Now your hand can keep up with your mind. No more forgetting a thought because you had to finish writing out the one before it.

4. There's no right or wrong way to map your mind. Whatever comes out on the page has to make sense only to you.

5. The order in which the thoughts fall on the page doesn't matter. The important thing is to be able to see them all at once.

6. Lets you be creative. Because mindmapping is so fast—less than two minutes for most memos and letters—you can let your mind go, see where it leads you. You will discover that your most creative solutions and most creative expressions of those solutions come when you follow your mind.

E. Once your thoughts are down on the page, you can order them into an outline.

Freewriting

Freewriting is to writing what mindmapping is to thinking. No other writing technique can help you get the words on the page faster or with more power.

Here's how freewriting works:

1. **Set a five-minute time limit.** Studies have shown that the most effective writing is done in short, little spurts with frequent breaks in between. So, write for five minutes, get a cup of coffee; write for five minutes, stare at the ceiling for a few seconds, write for five minutes, take a walk around your desk. You will get more words on the page and the quality of those words will be better than if you sit down and try not to get up until the assignment is finished.

2. **Write without stopping.** Not even for a second. Once your fingers touch those keys or your pen hits that page, write until your five-minute period is up. If you run out of things to say, write "I can't think of anything to say. I can't think of anything to say. I can't think of anything to say." You won't have to write that more than three times because writing anything else will be better.

3. **Write as quickly as you can.** But make it legible. Don't worry about spelling, punctuation, or grammar. They only slow you down. Resist the impulse to go back to put in a comma or to correct a misspelled word. What's important here is not the final product—it's the process of getting your words down on paper. So open the gates. Let the words pour out of your mind and onto the page. Don't be afraid to take some risks now, when there are no penalties. What comes out may not always be good, but freewriting offers you the best chances to produce quality writing.

Here's the result of one freewriting exercise:

> Freewriting is for you and no one else. It's a chance to say what you want like you want to say it without worrying about what anyone else might think. Even if the thoughts aren't whole sentences or they don't make sense you can get rid of the bad stuff later. Freewriting beats traditional writing because you're not always stopping to edit your right brain doesn't always have to fight it out with your left brain. That just slows you down. And the purpose of this is to put the sentences on the paper just the way you think. You can always edit the words later once their down there.

Freewriting From a Mindmap

Mindmapping and freewriting go hand in hand. First, you mindmap. Once your thoughts are on paper where you can see them all at once, you order them into an outline. Then you begin freewriting. Put your fingers on the keys or your pencil on the page and tell yourself, "Ready, set, go." Start writing whatever comes to mind about that first thought, the one that will open your memo or letter. Once you've said everything you need to about that first thought, move on to the second thought in your outline. Repeat the process until you've completed whatever it is you are writing. Remember: each thought stands for a separate paragraph.

Freewriting from a mindmap helps you accomplish several things:

You get started faster. Instead of staring at a blank piece of paper or computer screen while trying to think of an opening sentence that will cover everything you want to say, start freewriting. Worry about your opening sentence after writing the rest of your memo or letter.

You'll be more creative. If, while you are freewriting, your mind goes off on a tangent, follow it. You will discover that your most creative solutions to problems and your most creative expressions of those solutions will come during the times when you go where your mind leads you. Your outline will keep your thoughts from straying too far.

You'll write better. Freewriting helps you to get out of the way of the words. It allows you to create your own means of expression without having to worry about being correct.

You'll revise better. When most people write, they tend to think about what they want to say, write it down, and try to do so correctly so they don't have to go back and write it again. You perform three separate brain functions at the same time—almost as difficult a task as there is. Mindmapping and freewriting, on the other hand, break writing down into parts you can handle one at a time. First you think; then you write. Once the words are on the page, they are much easier to work with. You may throw many of them away. That's okay. It's much easier to cut words out or move them around when they're in front of you than it is to create and correct them while they're still in your head.

You'll save time. People who mindmap and then freewrite discover that they cut their writing time in half. They finish the first two steps in the writing process while other writers are still struggling with their opening paragraphs.

POWER WRITING TIPS

1. To get started . . .

   - Avoid interruptions.

   - Do all your writing at one time.

   - Warm up with the easy stuff first.

   - Say out loud what you want to write.

   - Write to someone you know.

   - Break the material down, putting each idea on a separate index card.

   - Try a different routine.

   - Give up, for the time being.

2. Mindmap your ideas as an alternative to traditional outlining

3. Outline the ideas in your mindmap, or begin writing directly from it.

4. Freewriting is a writing process that helps writers get words on the page quickly.

2

Taking a Critical Look

Revising

The next step in the writing process is revising. You must consider each of the following: the opening sentence, each paragraph, every sentence, every phrase, and every word.

The Opening Sentence

Once your ideas are on paper, look at your opening sentence. Because it determines whether readers will read on, your opening sentence is often the most important.

Here are some suggestions for writing a good opening sentence:

Begin with the climax. Instead of telling readers about events in the order in which they happened, begin with the climax.

Begin with a quotation. People love to read them. If you're writing about a person, consider opening with that person's words.

Begin with a startling detail or fact. Something that's unusual will catch your reader's attention.

Begin with a question. Opening with a question involves the reader from the very first sentence.

Begin with an opinion. Don't preface it with "I think" or "I believe" or "in my opinion." You are the writer. Of course the opinion is yours.

Begin with a definition. Simply state your definition. Do not write, "The dictionary says . . ."

Begin with a prediction. Point to the consequences of a present situation by telling your reader what will happen and why your prediction will come true.

Begin with a description. Characterize the setting for an event or for a scene or drama without revealing immediately what you are talking about.

Begin with an anecdote. This should be something that illustrates your subject, not a gratuitous joke.

Begin with something ironic or humorous. This is tough to do in a sentence or two, but it's effective when it works. Test what you have written on a friend or colleague before sending it to your reader.

The Paragraphs

Make sure each paragraph flows logically into the next. Then ask yourself these questions:

- **Do I have more than one idea in each paragraph?** Underline the central message of each paragraph or, if the message is only implied, write it next to the paragraph. If you have more than one message, you have more than one idea in each paragraph.

- **Is the most important piece of information in the opening sentence of each paragraph?** Does it make you want to keep on reading?

- **Do I need a concluding sentence?** Not if each paragraph develops points in a series. In these cases, you may want to use your last sentence to raise a question that will be answered in the first sentence of your next paragraph.

The Sentences

Generally speaking, short sentences are better than long ones, especially if the information you're presenting is complicated. On the other hand, too many short sentences in a row sound choppy, as in the following paragraph:

> You received your order for a copy of Herman Melville's *Moby Dick*. Unfortunately, the book isn't ready yet. A strike in our printing department has caused a delay. The machinists are now back at work. Please accept our apologies. Your book will be mailed soon.

The Phrases

The more jargon, clichés, and bureaucratic phrases you eliminate, the better your quality of writing will be and the greater the number of people who will be able to read it easily.

> Here is what former IBM executive Tom Watson has to say on the subject:
>
> A foreign language has been creeping into many of the memos and letters I read, and I want your help in stamping it out.
>
> Nothing seems to get finished anymore—it gets "finalized." Things don't happen at the same time but "coincident with this action." People talk about taking a "commitment position," and then because of the "volatility of schedule changes," they will "decommit" so that our "posture vis a vis the database that needs sizing" will be able to "enhance competitive positions."
>
> This kind of writing may be acceptable among bureaucrats, but not in this company. IBM wasn't built with fuzzy ideas and pretentious language. IBM was built with clear thinking and plain talk. Let's keep it that way.

The Words

The most effective words are your own, the ones you speak every day. You have tested these words in person and on the phone; you know how others respond when you use them. These are the words your reader wants to hear. Tom Watson's memo demonstrates the difference between memos written the way you speak and memos written like the one that follows:

> Operationally, teaching effectiveness is measured by assessing the levels of agreement between the perceptions of instructors and students on the rated ability of specific instructional behavior attributes which were employed during the course instruction.

In short, be yourself when you write. Don't use a big word when a small one will do. Notice how the shorter words in the following pairs actually pack more of a punch:

accumulate (gather)

amalgamate (merge)

configuration (shape)

expeditious (fast)

interface (relate)

materialize (happen)

optimum (best)

subsequent (later)

utilize (use)

The memo in the previous example also depends on clichés to deliver the message. But the result is that the clichés muddle the message. Avoid them and your writing will sound fresh. Here are several clichés that litter business documents:

acknowledge the receipt of

do not hesitate to call

enclosed please find

gratefully acknowledge

It has come to our attention . . .

pursuant to our conversation

Proofreading

Proofreading Your Own Work

Put some time and distance between your writing and your proofreading. Consider doing all your freewriting in the morning and all your proofreading in the afternoon, or all your freewriting one day and all your proofreading the next. The more time and distance you can put between your writing and your proofreading, the more objective you will be.

Proofreading is not re-reading. It is a line-by-line analysis to ensure that what you've written is the way you want it to be. Place a blank sheet of paper over all but the last line. Read the bottom line backwards from right to left. This technique forces you to concentrate on one word at a time. What you are reading will not make any sense, but it doesn't have to because you're only looking for misspelled words and typographical errors. As you finish proofreading each line, move the blank piece of paper up to the next line. Reverse the process when you get to the top. Read from left to right to catch the words you left out or the ones that fooled your computer's "spellcheck" program, words such as "their" for "there" and "its" for "it's."

Finally, ask someone else to read what you've written, someone whose intelligence you respect or whom you know to be a good writer.

Proofreading for Others

Proofreading another person's work is not autopsy. You don't always have to find something wrong with everything you are asked to read. Your job is to help the writer say what he or she wants to say, even if you would say it differently.

Read. But not with a pen in your hand. The worst proofreaders are those who make corrections before they have found what their writers are trying to say. Read the whole piece through before making any changes. If you don't understand some of what you read, give the paper back to the writer and ask the writer what he or she had in mind. Understanding what the writer is trying to say and letting the writer make corrections can't be overemphasized.

As you read, *think*. Study, weigh, consider, and analyze.

- Does the opening sentence grab your attention?
- Do the middle paragraphs keep it?
- Does the end leave the reader with something to think about?
- Are there any dull phrases or unnecessary words?
- Is the writing grammatically correct?

Next, *listen*. It's so easy for proofreaders to do all the talking. Some proofreaders think it's their job to tell the writer what's wrong with the writing, but the truth is that the less talking you do as a proofreader, the more you'll help the writer discover his or her own mistakes. Ask the writer questions such as these:

- What's the purpose of the piece?
- Who is the reader?
- Does the opening sentence grab your interest?
- What do you like most about what you wrote?
- Do you have any plans for a next draft?
- What changes would you make?
- Are there any opposing arguments you may not have considered?

- What feeling are you left with at the end?
- Would you read more?
- Are there any questions left unanswered?
- Are you moved to act?

Your job as proofreader is to listen and get involved. Don't worry about whether you like what you read. That's not important. If you pose your corrections as mild questions, you invite the writer to respond. Your most important task as a proofreader is to show the writer that you're on his or her side. If you can't do that, nothing else you say will have any effect.

How Writers and Proofreaders Can Help Each Other

Writers and proofreaders don't have to be best friends, but maintaining a professional relationship that's based on respect for each other's roles is essential to producing quality writing.

Here are a few ways writers can help proofers:

- Say something good about your proofreader.
- Ask for advice.
- Be open to suggestions.
- Be willing to take criticism.
- Don't think of your proofreader as a "butcher."

Here are a few suggestions proofreaders can follow to build their relationships with writers:

- Say something good about the writer.
- Don't judge in advance.
- Be willing to admit that you might learn something.
- Make suggestions without insisting they be used.
- Don't think of the writer as a "hack."

DELETE

check   ofyfice   Mr.   editting

ADD

chck   ofice   M.   editng

TRANSPOSE

chcek   ofice   Mr   editthg

MAKE LOWERCASE

check   office   MR.   EdiTing

MAKE UPPERCASE

Skillpath   mr.   new York   buddha

CLOSE UP SPACE

Skill Path   of fice   Mr .   edit ing

ADD SPACE

NewYork   officebuilding   Mr.Jones   BillyJoel

NEW PARAGRAPH

The managers who attended last week's meeting were
satisfied with Jack's report. Next week, we will
discuss three new topics.

POWER WRITING TIPS

1. After writing your piece, you must revise it. This involves taking a critical look at all the elements of your document:

   - The opening sentence
   - The paragraphs
   - Every sentence
   - Each word

2. Next, proofread your work, reading it line for line for misspelled words and typographical errors.

3. When you proofread for others, *think* and *listen.*

3

Developing a Style

Have you ever called someone on the phone and before saying who you were, the person you were speaking to called you by your name? It happens all the time. Why? Because you have your own individual speaking style. This style—the words you use and the ways you say them—separates your voice from all the others out there. It's as unique as your fingerprint.

You also have a writing style that separates you from everyone else, but because you were taught to imitate other people's voices ("pursuant to our telephone conversation," "in reference to your letter," "as per your request"), you never had the opportunity to discover and develop your own natural writing voice.

What is your natural writing voice? It is the same as your natural speaking voice. The closer you can get your writing to the way you speak, the more lively, powerful, and engaging it will be. But this does not mean that you should use slang or other unconventional words anymore than you should use clichés or jargon.

People have many different speaking voices. You probably have one voice when you speak to your friends and another voice when you speak to colleagues. You have one voice for speaking to your supervisors and another for speaking about your supervisor. If you're writing to a colleague, use the same words you would use if you were speaking to that colleague. If you are writing to a boss or supervisor, write in the voice that you would use if you were speaking to that person. Your natural writing voice allows you to write without ever losing the professional tone or lowering the standard level of English that is expected in your memos, letters, reports, and proposals.

Styles to Avoid

The message you send is shaped as much by your style as by the words you choose and your ability to follow grammatical rules. The following styles tend to turn readers off.

The Snotty

Inflated with false notions of their own importance, these writers want to show off. What they really do is reveal their own insecurity. Consider the following passages:

> Had the protagonist known beforehand that guppies lack a hypothalamus structure and can consequently be overfed, Raymond's love for his father's fish would not have resulted in their demise.

> Regardless of the fact that the protagonist's ignorance, then, is the root cause of the disproportion which exists between his good intentions (feeding the fish) and the reality those intentions encounter (their death), the disproportion between the two enables the protagonist to be both innocent and guilty at the same time.

The Arrogant or Unnecessarily Aggressive

These writers fail to consider the feelings of others. Almost every paragraph of the memos and letters they write could begin with the words, "Only an idiot would think . . ."

The Flippant

The flippant writer fails to take serious things seriously. Consider this message sent to the head of a local union who was recuperating from a heart attack:

The Board met last night and voted 18 to 12 in favor of your full recovery.

No matter how sure you are of your opinions or facts, common sense dictates that you respect your readers and put them at ease.

Rules to Avoid

You probably remember several hard-and-fast "unbreakable" rules from elementary and high school English classes. The truth is, you can break many of these rules and still produce good, quality writing.

Never Repeat a Word

There's some truth to this rule, but there's also another truth. Sometimes by repeating a word or a phrase or a sentence, you can make your messages even more powerful. Imagine if Abraham Lincoln had written "Of the people, by the persons, and for all the men, women and children."

Never End a Sentence in a Preposition

Do you end sentences in prepositions when you speak? All the time, probably. Then you can end sentences in prepositions when you write too. Winston Churchill made us realize how ridiculous this rule is when he told a reporter that ending his sentences in a preposition was "something up with which he would not put."

Never Split an Infinitive

Why not? Sometimes by breaking a rule, you can call greater attention to your message: Consider this line from Richard Andersen's *Writing That Works:* "You've been told to never split an infinitive, but if you're going to split one, isn't putting the absolute 'never' between 'to' and 'split' a good way to do it?"

Never Use the Word "I"

If you have done something personally for the reader, use the word "I," never the word "we." Mark Twain tells us there are only three kinds of people in the whole world who can use "we" when they mean "I": royalty, editors, and people with tapeworms.

Rules are effective only if they help make your messages clear. Otherwise, they just get in the way. In addition to asking yourself "Is it correct?" ask "Does it work?" There's often a big difference between writing "correctly" and writing well.

Never Begin a Sentence With a Conjunction

Beginning an occasional sentence with "and" or "but" helps to emphasize your message.

> People around the country have benefited from this discovery. And you can too.

The key here is not to overdo it and start too many sentences with a conjunction. Your sentences will sound choppy and, just as when you overuse the exclamation point, your emphasis will be lost on readers.

Language to Avoid

You can inadvertently tarnish your message by choosing certain words and phrases that have negative connotations.

Euphemisms

These are words people say when they want to hide something. You call the bombing of civilians, for example, "pacification" and the name of our biggest missile "Peacekeeper." George Orwell warns us to beware of people whose words do not bring a mental picture to our minds. "Protecting the peace" does not bring to mind the image of a bound prisoner kneeling before a cocked pistol.

Doubletalk

Doubletalkers avoid an issue by talking around it. *The New York Times* recently reported the story of an attorney defending three police officers accused of torturing prisoners to force confessions from them. "It was not done to deprive them of their liberty or to harm them," the attorney told the court, "but only for the purpose of recovering stolen property."

Sexism

Do you refer to men as "men" and women as "girls"? By using words like "repairman" and "salesman," do you perpetuate the idea that women are not fit for certain kinds of work? If so, you need some sensitivity training in the effects of discrimination through language. Meanwhile, you can avoid offending others by practicing the following guidelines as you write:

Use parallel language. Instead of writing "men and ladies," write "men and women" or "ladies and gentlemen."

Include both sexes. Instead of writing "mankind," write "people"; instead of "fireman," use "firefighter."

Use plural forms. Instead of writing "Each chairman must meet with his staff," write "Chairpersons must meet with their staffs."

Use "you." Instead of "Every police officer must prove himself," substitute "As a newly appointed police officer, you need to prove yourself."

Biased Language

Biased words show ignorance. They reveal the writer's biases towards people based on their race, age, religion, sexual orientation, and other factors.

Writers often contribute unknowingly to the biases in others by using closely related words in similar contexts. A "disability," for example, is a physical or emotional impairment; a "handicap" occurs when a person cannot overcome his or her disability. A person in a wheelchair is handicapped in certain situations; a person who has learned to overcome a reading disability is no longer handicapped.

Ten Ways to Win Over Your Readers

1. **Use short words.** They are the easiest to read and understand. Only insecure writers try to impress their readers with big words. Real writers know their job is not to impress but to express. If you write words such as the ones on the left-hand side of each of the lists below, consider substituting words like those in the parentheses:

   ascertain (find out)

   in the event that (if)

   disclose (show)

   locate (find)

   endeavor (try)

   obtain (get)

   forward (send)

   presently (now)

   inasmuch as (since)

   personnel (people)

2. **Use clear words.** Long and unfamiliar words only slow the reader down. Use words that are easy to pronounce and that everyone can immediately understand. Call a "pencil" a "pencil," not a "portable hand-held communications inscriber."

3. Use words correctly. The words that follow often are mistakenly used interchangeably. Some of the words most frequently misused in this way follow:

Affect. A verb meaning "to bring about a change, to substitute, to influence."

Effect. A noun meaning "a result" or a verb meaning "to cause."

Ensure. A verb meaning "to make certain, to guarantee."

Insure. A verb meaning "to protect with insurance against loss or damage."

It's. A verbal contraction meaning "it is" or "it has."

Its. A possessive pronoun meaning "belonging to it."

Fewer. An adjective dealing with numbers. (Fewer people attended.)

Less. An adjective dealing with quantity. (People eat less today.)

Lie. A verb meaning to rest or recline.

Lay. A verb meaning to put or place something down.

Try to. To "try to" means "to make an attempt."

Try and. To "try and" means that two separate actions are taking place: the "try" and whatever verb comes after it.

Disinterested. An adjective meaning "impartial."

Uninterested. An adjective meaning "not interested."

Some pronouns present problems for writers. "I" and "me" are frequently misused. As children, whenever you said "Jane and me want . . ." our parents corrected us. Because you were told to repeat "Jane and I" so many times, you now tend to use "I" any time you join it with someone else's name. What's the best way to tell when to use "I" or "me"? Read the sentence without the other person's name. For example, how would you complete the following sentence?

The secretary left without Jane and _____.

Would you use "I" or "me"? If you read the sentence without the other person's name, clearly the answer is "me."

"Myself" is another pronoun to be wary of. Most of the time it's either unnecessary or awkward. "I myself filed the report" is redundant. "The proposal submitted by Mike and myself" takes the perfectly good "me" out of the sentence and puts in its place the inflated, self-conscious "myself." In general, use "myself" only when the subject of the sentence is also the receiver of the action: "I washed myself."

4. **Use concrete words.** Words that say something are more effective. "Slums" creates a stronger image than "inner-city housing." "Beating children" tells us what "corporal punishment" really is. "Immature" is not nearly as effective as "forty going on ten."

5. Avoid unnecessary words. The more concise you are in your writing, the more power you preserve. Notice the energy that is lost when the words listed below have to carry the weight of those that have little meaning or are redundant:

basic	basic fundamentals
consensus	consensus of opinion
few	few in number
maximum	greatest maximum possible
until	until such time as

6. Write in the active voice. People speak in the active voice because it's short, clear, simple, direct, and easy to understand. "I expect to meet the deadline" has a ring of assertion that "The deadline is expected to be met" does not.

7. Use positive words. Consider the effect on the reader of the negative-sounding words in the following statements:

If you would only cooperate . . .

I cannot comprehend why . . .

You claim in your letter that . . .

Now, compare your reaction to these statements:

Congratulations!

I enjoyed talking with you the other day.

Thank you for your insightful and well-written proposal.

8. Use personal words. Don't be afraid to use words such as "you," "me," "I," "we," "us," and "they." These words are in fashion now. They have replaced the impersonal pronoun "one," as in "one must . . ." and "one shouldn't . . ."

9. **Use words that act.** Nouns derived from verbs have their place, but verbs are where the action is. For example, "The purpose of this company is the collection and distribution of information about real estate" is not nearly as powerful as "This company collects and distributes information about real estate."

Here are some more verbs you can free from the noun chains that bind them:

Verb	*Noun*
anticipate	anticipation
conclude	conclusion
establish	establishment
install	installation
object	objection
reveal	revelation

10. **Use a thesaurus.** But not to look up a new word. The thesaurus doesn't list words that are the same in meaning as the word you are looking up; it lists words that are similar in meaning. If you use the thesaurus to look up a new word, you run the risk of distorting what you mean to say. Use the thesaurus to look up a word you have forgotten or for a wider choice of words you already know.

Ten Ways to Lose Your Reader

1. Use abstract words. These words are no more solid than fat cut from a steak:

new avenues being explored

first and foremost

in-depth study

in this day and age

many and varied

multifaceted problem

more unique

for all intents

2. Use fad words. These words are picked up, worked to death, and abandoned quickly. They make you sound dated. Fast.

vital	interface
utilize	orientate
input	orchestrate
unique	facilitate

3. Be redundant. With redundant writers, if something is "essential," for example, it is also "absolutely essential." Other examples of redundancy include:

completely unanimous	combine together
small in size	positive gain
true fact	complete absence
clearly evident	modern life today

4. Use tired words. These words have been used so much they no longer have any impact. "Professional," "bottom line," and "give good meeting" are currently popular, but few words are called into service as much as "controversial." In a two-week period, editors at the *New York Times* discovered that stories about all the following subjects contained the word "controversial":

The suffragist Lucy Stone

A fumble by football player Allen Rice

Pet projects of influential legislators

A stamp honoring St. Francis of Assisi

The Vancouver Canucks' third-period goal

An endorsement by the National Organization of Women

A proposed assault by Israeli paratroopers

Canada's new energy program

Linda Rondstadt's new album

And that's fewer than half the stories!

5. Write two words as one. "A lot" and "all right" are the most commonly abused words in this category. You'd never write "alwrong," would you?

6. Use words that aren't words. There's no such word as "clichéd," for example. The word you probably want in this case is "cliché" or "trite," or one of its synonyms. Nor are there such words as "irregardless" and "reimplement," regardless of how many times they are implemented.

7. **Use unfamiliar words.** "Heuristics as a Concomitant to Learning Cognation Skills" was the title of a speech given at a conference for communication professors. Guess why only a handful of people showed up?

8. **Use the word "hopefully."** Few words upset the office grammarian or frustrate an English teacher as much as "hopefully" when it is used to express your own or someone else's hoping. Use "I hope" or "You hope." "Hopefully" is perfectly acceptable when it's used to mean "in a hopeful manner," as in this example:

   The child asked hopefully for a piece of candy.

9. **Keep from getting to the point.** Oliver Jensen tells us that if Dwight David Eisenhower had written "The Gettysburg Address," it would sound like this: "I haven't checked these figures, but around 90 years ago, I think it was, a number of individuals organized a governmental set-up here in this country—I believe it concerned the Eastern areas—with this idea they were following up based on a sort of national independence arrangement and the program that every individual is just as good as every other individual."

10. **Write above the reader's level of understanding.** Most of the stories appearing in *The New Yorker* and *The Atlantic Monthly* are written at a twelfth-grade reading level, but no one ever accused John Cheever, Woody Allen, and Anne Beatie & Co. of talking down to their readers. To test the reading level at which you write, put together enough of your writing to equal 150 words. Count the number of words with one syllable. Divide that number by ten. Then subtract your answer from twenty. The number you get is the number of years of education your readers need in order to understand what you've written without being burdened.

POWER WRITING TIPS

1. Your style is your natural writing voice, which is your natural speaking voice.

2. Avoid styles that turn readers off: snotty, arrogant, aggressive, and flippant.

3. Many longtime writing rules can be broken to make your style less formal and to emphasize your message.

4. Avoid language that "poisons" or otherwise detracts from your message: euphemisms, doubletalk, and sexist and biased language.

5. Win your readers over by keeping your writing concise, clear, and concrete.

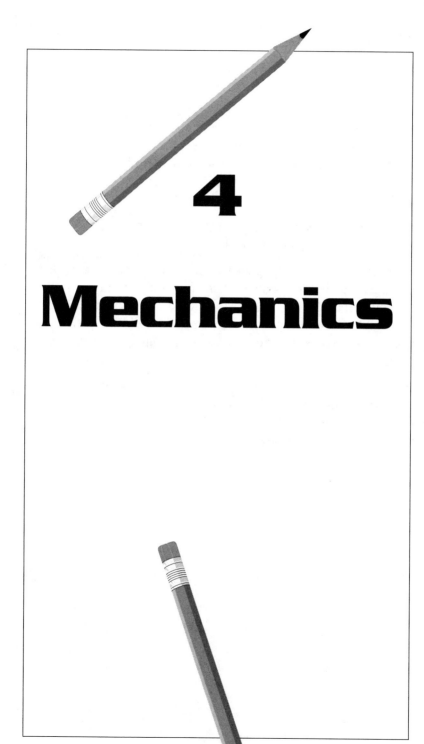

4

Mechanics

Not all the rules of spelling grammar and punctuation were created to make our lives miserable their job is to help us say what you want to say and to make it easier for our readers to understand our messages the spaces you make between our words are just as important as the words themselves

See where you'd be without punctuation? Imagine if you disregarded spelling and syntax as well.

Your supervisor and colleagues may not always praise writing that is correct, but they sure notice when yours isn't, don't they? And they often show all the other people in the office your creative new ways of constructing sentences or spelling old words. But what is "correct" or "incorrect" is not the province of any single guide to style.

How, then, do you resolve the conflict between you and the office grammarian? *Be yourself.* You speak in simple, clear, easy-to-understand sentences. If you write like you speak, much of what you write will "correct" itself.

Spelling

Of all the rules governing mechanics, none are so tyrannical as those governing spelling. There are just no gray areas here. Everything is either right or wrong. Nevertheless, here are a couple of ways you can cut down on your spelling mistakes:

Use the words you speak. Rarely will you say a word that you don't also know how to spell. Notice the degree of spelling difficulty that separates the kind of words you may tend to speak from the kind you tend to write:

after	subsequent
begin	commence
use	utilize
people	personnel
try	endeavor

List the words you can't spell. Every person has mental blocks against anywhere from five to twenty-five words. No matter how many times we look them up, we'll never be able to spell them correctly. Write these words on a piece of paper and tape it to the inside of your desk drawer. When the word comes up, open the drawer, copy the word, close the drawer, and forget about it. Many commonly misspelled words are included in the following list:

accidentally	maintenance	receive
acquaintance	miscellaneous	remuneration
argument	necessary	resemblance
attendance	noticeable	ridiculous
definite	occasion	separate
dependent	occurrence	succeed
exaggerate	offered	threshold
existence	omitted	truly
government	preceding	usually
judgment	privilege	withhold

Punctuation

Today, there are more than thirty punctuation marks. The good news is that you rarely use more than twelve of them. The bad news is that one of those twelve, the comma, gives us more trouble than all the others combined.

The Comma

Here are the most common instances in which commas are used:

1. Use a comma in front of the word that joins two sentences.

   John hit the ball, and Mary fielded it.

   John hit the ball, but Mary threw him out.

2. Use a comma to introduce something that is not a main part of the sentence.

   In addition to fielding the ball, Mary tagged the runner.

   Fielding the ball, Mary hurt her arm.

   Before Mary fielded the ball, she checked the runner at third.

3. Use a comma to separate items in a list.

   Mary brought the balls, the bats, and the gloves.

   If John is willing to work, make the necessary sacrifices, and get a pair of glasses, he may some day be as good as Mary.

4. Use a comma to separate the main sentence from its parts.

   Mary, the chief executive officer at Stanford and Bumstein, leads the nation in stolen bases.

   Mary, who leads the nation in stolen bases, also leads her team in RBIs.

5. Use commas to separate quotations from the rest of the sentence.

   Leo Durocher tells us, "Show me a good loser, and I'll show you a loser."

   "If my mother was rounding third base with the winning run against us," Leo Durocher once said, "I'd trip her."

   "Nice guys finish last," Leo Durocher told the press.

6. Use commas to separate words from those they are sometimes connected to.

   Brooklyn, New York, was the home of . . .

   On August 14th, 1955, the Dodgers . . .

The most common comma error is the comma splice. In a comma splice, the comma is made to do the work of a period. It joins two ideas that should be separated by a period, a semicolon, or a comma and a conjunction.

   He couldn't tolerate the noise, noise made him nervous.

This sentence should have been written:

   He couldn't tolerate the noise. Noise made him nervous.

or

   He couldn't tolerate the noise; noise made him nervous.

or

   He couldn't tolerate the noise, and noise made him nervous.

When in doubt, leave the comma out. Even the strictest grammarian can find all kinds of reasons why you might leave a comma out, but the minute you put one in where it doesn't belong it's wrong with a capital "W" every single time. This sentence left out two.

The Colon

There are only two main rules to remember about colons:

1. Use a colon as a lead in. A colon signals that what follows clarifies or defines whatever came before it:

   The chief soon discovered the cause of the fire: arson.

   The student narrowed his list to three writers: Alice Walker, Zora Neale Hurston, and James Baldwin.

2. Use a colon in the salutations of business letters.

   Dear Ms. Hemingway:

   Dear Michele:

   Michele:

The Semicolon

Many people avoid the semicolon, but it serves two useful purposes.

1. Use the semicolon to join two closely related sentences. Notice how, in the following example, the first sentence reads faster than the second.

   John hit the ball; he ran to first.

   John hit the ball. He ran to first.

   The first sentence reads faster because a semicolon doesn't signal as great a pause as a period.

2. Use the semicolon to separate series of items containing commas.

   The players packed their uniforms; balls, bats, and gloves; and training equipment.

The Hyphen

The hyphen is generally used to show a close relationship among words.

1. Use the hyphen to join closely related adjectives.

   Newport has a mile-long beach.

   The lifeguards wear apple-red shorts.

2. Use the hyphen to connect compound nouns and verbs.

   Her mother-in-law attended the ceremony.

   Please single-space the letter to the vendor.

3. Use a hyphen to add a prefix that forms a word that could be confused with a similarly spelled word.

   re-cover

   recover

The Dash

Dashes are a popular punctuation mark right now.

1. Many people use them to replace colons.

   The student narrowed his list to three writers—Alice Walker, Zora Neale Hurston, and James Baldwin.

2. Dashes can also take the place of parentheses:

   Many readers—unless they favor Alice Walker—favor Zora Neale Hurston.

3. The best use of the dash, however, is to show hesitation—as an aside or afterthought or clarification—before going on with the rest of the sentence.

Grammar

Grammar involves the way you arrange words when you write or speak. If you are a native speaker of English, you know all you need to know about how to structure a sentence. You have been structuring sentences all your life. As long as you write as closely as possible to the way you speak, you will almost always arrange your words in simple, clear, easy-to-understand prose. Those few times when you don't probably involve the common syntactical problems covered in this chapter.

Subject-Verb Agreement

You all know that the subject and verb have to agree in number; that is, singular subjects require singular verbs and plural subjects must have plural verbs.

> He does not care.

> They do not care.

But sometimes you put so many words between the subject and verb that you become confused. You make the verb agree with the last noun you wrote, as in this sentence:

> Bob's working habits, like his way of organizing a letter, leaves something to be desired.

If you make this error frequently, put your left finger on the subject of every long sentence you write. Put your right finger on the first verb that comes along. If the subject and the verb agree in number, you've probably written the sentence correctly.

Even when you correctly identify the subject and verb, however, there are a few words that always give us trouble: "each," "anyone," "anybody," "no one," "nobody," "everyone," "everybody," "someone," "somebody." These words all require singular verbs.

> Each has . . .
>
> Someone wants to . . .
>
> Nobody needs to . . .

When one subject is singular and the other is plural and they are joined by "or," the verb agrees in number with the closest subject.

> The pitcher or the outfielders were selected for the honor.

Noun and Pronoun Agreement

The rule is simple: Make nouns and pronouns agree in number and gender. The application of the rule is tough, however. Although all nouns and pronouns have a number and a gender, only nouns are written in the third person. Pronouns can be written in the first person ("I," "you"), second person ("you"), or third person ("he," "she," "it," "they," "one," "some," "none").

Try to make your nouns and pronouns agree in number, gender, and person. A second-person pronoun should not be linked with a third-person noun:

> The scouts took so much equipment the campsite looked like you never left your living room.

This sentence should read:

> The scouts took so much equipment the campsite looked like they never left their living rooms.

Modifiers: Dangling and Misplaced

Dangling modifiers do not relate correctly to their subjects:

> Refusing to be inducted into the army, the World Boxing Association stripped him of his title.

The previous sentence says the World Boxing Association was drafted. It should read:

> Refusing to be inducted into the army, he was stripped of his title.

or

> The World Boxing Association stripped him of his title for refusing to be drafted into the army.

Misplaced modifiers lead to misreadings:

> She paid $50 for a dress at Saks that she despised.

Is it Saks or the dress that she despises? Depending on your answer, the sentence should read:

> At Saks, which she despises, she paid $50 for a dress.

or

> She paid $50 at Saks for a dress she despises.

Fragments and Run-ons

Fragments are incomplete thoughts. Sometimes a subject or a verb may be missing. Sometimes the subject and verb are there, but another word such as "who" or "although" indicates that something is missing. The thought cannot stand by itself. "Although John was taller than Mary" is an example of this kind of fragment.

Although you speak in justified fragments all the time, you're not very good at writing them. To test whether your fragment is justifiable, read it out loud within the context in which it appears. Here's a dialogue of perfectly acceptable fragments. Notice, however, that none of these sentences would be possible without the first, complete sentence:

"Where are you going tonight?"

"To the movies."

"Who with?"

"Nobody."

"What time?"

"Now."

Run-on sentences are two complete thoughts that have been joined together without the proper punctuation or a proper connecting word:

I know what I'm saying I just finished the book.

This sentence should read:

I know what I'm saying. I just finished the book. (Use a period or a semicolon between two complete thoughts.)

or

I know what I'm saying because I just finished the book. (Join the two sentences with a connecting word.)

or

Because I just finished reading the book, I know what I'm saying. (Make one of the thoughts subordinate to the other.)

Three Ways to Eliminate Mechanical Errors

1. **Write as closely as possible to the way you speak.** We speak in simple, clear, easy-to-understand sentences. These sentences are very easy to construct. If you write like you speak and use the words you say, you'll make fewer mechanical errors.

2. **Proofread out loud.** The importance of reading out loud cannot be overemphasized. Our ears make excellent editors; our eyes don't. If you're not sure about the way a sentence is constructed, read it out loud.

3. **Ask someone else to correct your work.** When your reader returns your work, make a list of your mistakes. Then give your reader another piece of your writing to correct. When you get the second piece back, add the mistakes you made in it to the list you began with the first piece. Repeat this process for about five or six writing samples, each time adding to your list of mistakes. But don't just list your new mistakes. List every single mistake every single time and watch for a pattern to develop.

The same two or three mistakes will keep reappearing. Once you have identified the two or three mistakes you are most likely to make, use the appropriate sections of this book to find out how to correct them. In the future, all you have to do is proofread out loud and be aware of the two or three mistakes you are most likely to make.

POWER WRITING TIPS

1. Reduce your spelling mistakes by writing only words that you would speak and keeping a list of words you have trouble spelling.

2. Concentrate on the basic rules of punctuation and you'll have no trouble with most written business communications. You can always consult a reference book for the finer points, if necessary.

3. Believe it or not, most grammar rules are second nature to you because you're a native speaker of English. Watch for these trouble spots: subject-verb agreement, noun and pronoun agreement, dangling and misplaced modifiers, sentence fragments, and run-ons.

4. Eliminate mechanical errors by writing like you speak, proofreading aloud, and asking someone else to check your work.

5

Writing That Means Business

The principles of good writing—that it be clear, simple, and easy to understand—stay the same no matter what you're writing. Only the forms—business, technical, or academic—change. Clear writing reflects a clear mind; muddled writing reflects a muddled one. In short, there's no reason to make your messages unintelligible:

> Among the additional functional enhancements of the support program are dynamic reconfigurations.

Just because you may work for an institution is no reason you have to sound like one. Phrases such as "prioritized evaluative procedures" and "modified departmental agenda" only make readers work hard and resent you. In an increasingly dehumanizing age, people look for people who communicate easily. Writers who come across as people rather than as machines are going to make the best impressions, win the most customers, and earn the most money. You may even find a friend.

Here are some pointers for some of the most frequently used forms of writing.

Memos

Before writing any memo, ask yourself:

Would it be better to call? Most memos are too long, sent to too many people, and written by people who write too many of them. They also take time and energy. Many times, speaking, which is more personal and less formal, works better.

On the other hand, memos force us to articulate our thoughts, eliminate hearsay, reach any number of people simultaneously, keep us from repeating ourselves, get our name seen, make sure you get credit for ideas, and when they are well written, keep us off the phone and busy doing other things.

Who am I writing to? The answer is not merely the name of the reader. What does the reader do? What are the reader's professional interests? What kinds of evidence appeal to the reader? What will make this reader support my recommendations or follow my suggestions?

What do I want to say? You probably know what you want to say in any memo you write, but you would be surprised how often writers don't say specifically what they want the reader to do. How much does the reader know about the subject? What questions might the reader ask? What objections might the reader have? What will help the reader understand better what I want him or her to do?

When do I want it done? Saying specifically "when" is just as important as "what" if you want your readers to act promptly and efficiently. When do you need a response by, and why is it important to have a response by this time? The reader will respond better if given a reason.

Letters

Business letters, like any other kind of writing, deliver two messages. The first is its literal message; the second is the impression it makes on the reader. To get your reader's best response:

Consider a subject line. Subject lines not only call attention to what's important in the letter, they are visually inviting for your reader.

Call your reader by name. Letters written to specific people are answered faster and more effectively than letters written to whoever happens to open the mail. If you spell your reader's name correctly, you have the reader on your side before he or she begins to read the first word.

Make it look good. Make sure the margins are even, your message is centered, there are no correction marks, and you've used high-quality stationery.

Keep it short. Busy people don't have time to read longwinded letters. Nor do they have time to read chatty paragraphs that have nothing to do with the subject of the letter.

Be correct. If your letters contain mistakes, your readers will have only one of two reactions: they'll think you're either stupid or lazy. Make every letter as close to perfect as you can.

Sign your name so people can read it. Malcolm Forbes tells us the biggest work of ego is an illegible signature.

Handwrite the postscript. Studies have shown that handwritten postscripts are often read twice: when the reader opens the letter and when the reader finishes the letter.

Reports

The key to writing a successful report is to write the beginning last.

When we read, we process information differently from when we write, or at least we want our information given to us in a different way. When we write, we follow a logical, natural, usually chronological pattern: this happened, then this happened, and these are the conclusions I have reached based on what happened. When we read, however, we want the conclusion first. We want to know the point, the theme, the direction we're going in before we start. Readers who have to wade through a series of events or issues before reaching the conclusion often aren't sure if it agrees with what preceded it. They have to go back and re-read the report to see if every event or issue points to the conclusion.

Freewrite in the natural way, moving from the details to the conclusion. Then move your conclusion to the opening of your report. Now your readers know the purpose and direction of the report. They can see, as they read through the details, whether what you say agrees with your conclusion. And just so there's no mistake about what you conclude, consider repeating the conclusion at the end of the report—only in slightly different words so it won't sound like you're repeating yourself word for word.

After you have finished freewriting your report and moving your conclusion to the beginning, ask yourself these questions:

Is your report entirely self-contained? Make sure your readers are aware of all important memos, letters, and other reports. No one appreciates having to search for documentation that should have been provided.

Does your report present your findings clearly? The decision makers want to know what you have concluded and what you recommend—and they want it up front. Presenting your summary first is what separates writer-based prose from reader-based prose.

Have you anticipated your readers' responses? What do they know and what do they need to know? What are their attitudes toward the subject? How will your report affect your relationship with them?

Proposals

What is true about reports is also true of proposals. The major difference between reports and proposals, however, is that in proposals you are trying to persuade your readers to follow your recommendations. You want to convince your readers that they need what you suggest. To succeed you must:

Respect your readers. Don't talk down to them because you think you have the answer to their problem. Accept the fact that they might disagree with you for reasons other than their stupidity or negative attitudes. You can keep your readers' personalities from playing a part in your proposal by focusing on the issues and avoiding the personal pronouns "you" and "I" that are so effective in other kinds of writing.

Begin where you can agree. If you know some of your readers are going to object to your proposal, weaken their barriers by focusing early on your points of agreement.

Anticipate objections. Even the illogical ones. "You've never done it that way" and "If you do it for you, you have to do it for everybody" and "You don't want to set a precedent" may not make sense to you, but they are lifelines to people who fear change.

Time your proposal. Consider waiting until your readers recognize a need for what you propose, or at least make it clear that there will soon be a need if they don't act on what you say.

Submit your proposal when your readers aren't pressed by other needs. If your reader has already accepted a competing recommendation, wait until it fails before submitting yours, or tailor your proposal to meet any weaknesses in the accepted solution.

POWER WRITING TIPS

1. The principles of good writing remain the same no matter what form your writing takes.

2. The most common forms of written business communications are memos, letters, reports, and proposals. Make sure you know the elements essential to making each one a written success.

You Can't Grow on Fear . . .

You will never grow as a writer if you allow your fears of the writing process to overcome you.

Here's what fear will do to you:

Fear of failure. The result is writing by formula. Taking risks might involve more editing, but improved writing is impossible without them.

Fear of asking difficult questions. The result is writing that has no depth.

Fear of doing research. The result is incomplete data and frustrated readers.

Fear of writing short sentences. The result is writing that often doesn't mean what it says or says what it doesn't mean.

Fear of admitting a mistake. The result is a writer who never learns anything.

Fear of double-checking. The result exposes a writer's poor note-taking ability or inaccuracy.

Fear of talking about your subject before you write about them. The result is that no one knows how little you know until they read what you have to say.

Fear of putting out. The result is a lost opportunity to make a good impression.

Fear of reading other writers. The result is a prose style that never changes, never develops, and never leads the reader to expect something new.

Don't Take It Personally

Finally, to get past your fears, learn not take criticism personally.

Consider what critics had to say about these well-known writers.

On Emily Bronte's *Wuthering Heights:*

Here all the faults of *Jane Eyre* by Charlotte Bronte are magnified a thousand fold, and the only consolation that you have in reflecting upon it is that it will never be generally read.

—North British Review

On Anton Chekhov's *Uncle Vanya:*

If you were to ask me what *Uncle Vanya* is about, I would say about as much as I can take.

—Journal American

On William Faulkner's *Absalom, Absalom!:*

The final blowup of what was once a remarkable, if minor, talent.

—The New Yorker

On Ernest Hemingway's *For Whom the Bell Tolls:*

At a conservative estimate, one million dollars will be spent by American readers for this book. They will get 34 pages of permanent value. Mr. Hemingway: please publish the massacre scene separately, and then forget *For Whom the Bell Tolls;* please leave stories of the Spanish Civil War to Malraux.

—Commonweal

On William Shakespeare's *Othello:*

Pure melodrama. There is not a touch of characterization that goes below the skin.

—George Bernard Shaw, *Saturday Review*

On John Steinbeck's *Of Mice and Men:*

Of Mice and Men will appeal to sentimental critics and cynical sentimentalists. Readers less easily thrown off their trolly will still prefer Hans Christian Andersen.

—*Time*

On Virginia Woolf's *To The Lighthouse:*

Her work is poetry; it must be judged as poetry, and all the weaknesses of poetry are inherent in it.

—New York Evening Post

Bibliography and Suggested Reading

Andersen, Richard. *Writing That Works: A Practical Guide for Business and Creative People.* New York: McGraw-Hill, 1989.

Corbett, Edward. *The Little English Handbook.* Glenview, Ill.: Scott, Foresman, 1987.

Elbow, Peter. *Writing Without Teachers.* New York: Oxford University Press, 1973.

Fowler, Gene. *Modern English Usage.* New York: Oxford University Press, 1926.

Hall, Donald. *Writing Well.* Boston: Little, Brown, 1976.

Strunk, William, Jr., and E.B. White. *The Elements of Style.* New York: Macmillan, 1959.

Available From
SkillPath Publications

Self-Study Sourcebooks

Climbing the Corporate Ladder: What You Need to Know and Do to Be a Promotable Person *by Barbara Pachter and Marjorie Brody*

Coping With Supervisory Nightmares: 12 Common Nightmares of Leadership and What You Can Do About Them *by Michael and Deborah Singer Dobson*

Defeating Procrastination: 52 Fail-Safe Tips for Keeping Time on Your Side *by Marlene Caroselli, Ed.D.*

Discovering Your Purpose *by Ivy Haley*

Going for the Gold: Winning the Gold Medal for Financial Independence *by Lesley D. Bissett, CFP*

Having Something to Say When You Have to Say Something: The Art of Organizing Your Presentation *by Randy Horn*

Info-Flood: How to Swim in a Sea of Information Without Going Under *by Marlene Caroselli, Ed.D.*

The Innovative Secretary *by Marlene Caroselli, Ed.D.*

Letters & Memos: Just Like That! *by Dave Davies*

Mastering the Art of Communication: Your Keys to Developing a More Effective Personal Style *by Michelle Fairfield Poley*

Obstacle Illusions: Coverting Crisis to Opportunity *by Marlene Caroselli, Ed.D.*

Organized for Success! 95 Tips for Taking Control of Your Time, Your Space, and Your Life *by Nanci McGraw*

A Passion to Lead! How to Develop Your Natural Leadership Ability *by Michael Plumstead*

P.E.R.S.U.A.D.E.: Communication Strategies That Move People to Action *by Marlene Caroselli, Ed.D.*

Productivity Power: 250 Great Ideas for Being More Productive *by Jim Temme*

Promoting Yourself: 50 Ways to Increase Your Prestige, Power, and Paycheck *by Marlene Caroselli, Ed.D.*

Proof Positive: How to Find Errors Before They Embarrass You *by Karen L. Anderson*

Risk-Taking: 50 Ways to Turn Risks Into Rewards *by Marlene Caroselli, Ed.D. and David Harris*

Stress Control: How You Can Find Relief From Life's Daily Stress *by Steve Bell*

The Technical Writer's Guide *by Robert McGraw*

Total Quality Customer Service: How to Make It Your Way of Life *by Jim Temme*

Write It Right! A Guide for Clear and Correct Writing *by Richard Andersen and Helene Hinis*

Your Total Communication Image *by Janet Signe Olson, Ph.D.*

Handbooks

The ABC's of Empowered Teams: Building Blocks for Success *by Mark Towers*

Assert Yourself! Developing Power-Packed Communication Skills to Make Your Points Clearly, Confidently, and Persuasively *by Lisa Contini*

Breaking the Ice: How to Improve Your On-the-Spot Communication Skills *by Deborah Shouse*

The Care and Keeping of Customers: A Treasury of Facts, Tips, and Proven Techniques for Keeping Your Customers Coming BACK! *by Roy Lantz*

Challenging Change: Five Steps for Dealing With Change *by Holly DeForest and Mary Steinberg*

Dynamic Delegation: A Manager's Guide for Active Empowerment *by Mark Towers*

Every Woman's Guide to Career Success *by Denise M. Dudley*

Exploring Personality Styles: A Guide for Better Understanding Yourself and Your Colleagues *by Michael Dobson*

Grammar? No Problem! *by Dave Davies*

Great Openings and Closings: 28 Ways to Launch and Land Your Presentations With Punch, Power, and Pizazz *by Mari Pat Varga*

Hiring and Firing: What Every Manager Needs to Know *by Marlene Caroselli, Ed.D. with Laura Wyeth, Ms.Ed.*

How to Be a More Effective Group Communicator: Finding Your Role and Boosting Your Confidence in Group Situations *by Deborah Shouse*

How to Deal With Difficult People *by Paul Friedman*

Learning to Laugh at Work: The Power of Humor in the Workplace *by Robert McGraw*

Making Your Mark: How to Develop a Personal Marketing Plan for Becoming More Visible and More Appreciated at Work *by Deborah Shouse*

Meetings That Work *by Marlene Caroselli, Ed.D.*

The Mentoring Advantage: How to Help Your Career Soar to New Heights *by Pam Grout*

Minding Your Business Manners: Etiquette Tips for Presenting Yourself Professionally in Every Business Situation *by Marjorie Brody and Barbara Pachter*

Misspeller's Guide *by Joel and Ruth Schroeder*

Motivation in the Workplace: How to Motivate Workers to Peak Performance and Productivity *by Barbara Fielder*

NameTags Plus: Games You Can Play When People Don't Know What to Say *by Deborah Shouse*

Networking: How to Creatively Tap Your People Resources *by Colleen Clarke*

New & Improved! 25 Ways to Be More Creative and More Effective *by Pam Grout*

Power Write! A Practical Guide to Words That Work *by Helene Hinis*

The Power of Positivity: Eighty ways to energize your life *by Joel and Ruth Schroeder*

Putting Anger to Work For You *by Ruth and Joel Schroeder*

Reinventing Your Self: 28 Strategies for Coping With Change *by Mark Towers*

Saying "No" to Negativity: How to Manage Negativity in Yourself, Your Boss, and Your Co-Workers *by Zoie Kaye*

The Supervisor's Guide: The Everyday Guide to Coordinating People and Tasks *by Jerry Brown and Denise Dudley, Ph.D.*

Taking Charge: A Personal Guide to Managing Projects and Priorities *by Michal E. Feder*

Treasure Hunt: 10 Stepping Stones to a New and More Confident You! *by Pam Grout*

A Winning Attitude: How to Develop Your Most Important Asset! *by Michelle Fairfield Poley*

For more information, call 1-800-873-7545.

Notes

Notes

Notes

Notes